INTRODUCTION

Most people are familiar with the general term "parrot," but only those with a more detailed knowledge of this fascinating group of birds know what a lory or lorikeet is. Those who see a lorikeet for the first time will have no difficulty in recognizing it as a parrot because it has the typical stocky type, the hooked bill, the lovebirds, African Grey Parrots, macaws, cockatoos, conures and cockatiels will all subsist on a simple seed diet; lories and lorikeets will not. They require a much more fluid feeding regimen consisting of pollen, nectar, and fruits. This fact has given these birds an undeserved reputation for being somewhat dirty, foul-

Before purchasing a lory, some research on the various species available should be done. Pictured here are two Rainbow Lories, *T.h. flavicans*.

bright colors generally associated with parrots, and the typical climbing ability common to all such birds.

Lories and lorikeets differ from the majority of parrots in a very unique way. Their dietary needs are exclusive from the rest of the parrot family. The budgerigar of Australia, Amazon parrots, smelling, and, most important, difficult to maintain in good health. In reality, lories and lorikeets are very clean birds with especially immaculate plumage; many are very reliable breeders and all are amusing, affectionate, and highly intelligent. They are also more colorful than the majority of parrot species, and have much to offer the potential bird keeper or breeder.

To those thinking of purchasing one of these beautiful birds, it must be stated from the beginning that they do need a little extra care and attention because of the fact that their diet is basically liquid. This means that their feces are liquid as well, and it becomes obvious that unless this is fully

with short tails (lories), and those with long tails (lorikeets). Such terms are useful references for everyday use but have no particular scientific basis; in this book the terms lory and lorikeet are used in a general sense and they refer to either the long-or short-tailed members of the family Loriidae.

Over the last few decades the

Lories differ from other parrot-like birds in that they lack the muscular gizzard necessary for digesting seeds. Shown is a Rainbow Lory.

appreciated, the birds quickly appear dirty and the feces become a source of problem. Attempts to convert them to a seed diet are ill-advised because nature did not equip them to cope with such foods. They would quickly become ill if given only seed as a staple diet.

The terms "lory" and "lorikeet" are avicultural and are used to distinguish between those species

lories have been rather neglected as avicultural subjects due to their diet. With much improved knowledge of their needs, and greater availability of commercial food preparations, this situation is changing rapidly. The value of all parrot-like birds has been rising at a considerable rate because of the fact that as a group, they are far more subjected to survival problems in the wild

The Dusky Lory, *Pseudeos fuscata*, belongs to a monotypic genus. It is said to be closely related to species of the genus *Eos*, but varies by the tail being noticably smaller, and there is bare skin surrounding the lower mandible.

(due to habitat destruction) than most other bird groups. This has encouraged more people than in the past to attempt breeding their birds, and so species such as the lories, have gained from both extra promotion and greater availability of domestically bred birds.

This book contains sufficient information to maintain these birds in a healthy condition, and to breed them if desired. It will provide the basic platform of knowledge to which the reader can add both practical experience and reference from other, more detailed books.

Dusky Lory. More and more bird keepers have become interested in learning the proper means to care for these birds, and many captive breeding programs have begun.

ACCOMMODATIONS

As far as housing goes, lories represent a challenge to their potential owners, especially if the birds are to be kept as indoor pets. Lories are birds with the strength associated with parrots, yet they share in the dietary needs of those birds called "softbilled," birds that need soft or liquid diets as their staple food. The typical parrot cage is not constructed for lories, nor is the one produced for softbilled birds. This means owners must either prepare their own cage (or have someone else do it) or they must modify the larger parrot cage (which will probably be less economical than making one's own). From the aviary viewpoint, lories might actually be easier to cater to than numerous other parrot species of similar size.

The type of accommodation you choose for your lory must have plenty of room for it to move about, and must take into account the bird's dietary needs of a liquid diet.

CAGES

Accommodation for lories kept as household pets must take account of two factors. First, it must allow the bird(s) plenty of room to move about. Secondly, it must take account of the feeding habits of these birds. Because of their high cost, many pet owners purchase parrot cages that are just too small for the birds, but no cage can ever be too large for a cage bird. The height of the cage must be such that the clearance room above the bird's head, when it is on its highest perch, is about 15cm (6in) minimum. The space between the bird's tail-tip and the floor should be at least 23cm (9in). The width should be such that the bird can fully extend its wings in order to exercise. The length of the cage can be the same as the width. Such a cage assumes that the bird is given plenty of free-flying time outside of its accommodation so that the cage is merely a place for it to feed and sleep in. Lories normally sleep in their nests in the wild, and it should be understood that any cage is far removed from natural conditions.

The cage materials (assuming a standard parrot cage) should be of the highest quality, and chromium plated metal is far better than galvanized metal, but it is much more expensive. The space between the bars must be such that the lory cannot escape, or even get its head stuck. Some cages are made with plastic bases which are easy to keep clean, but if the lory can get its beak on their sides, it will soon commence biting pieces off; if swallowed these could be very dangerous to its health. The sides of a standard parrot cage will need to have strips of strong sheet glass affixed from the bottom to a few inches up the cage, this is in order to reduce the amount of feces that are squirted out of the cage. Two strong perches should be fitted across the width of the cage at slightly differing heights. You can remove the perches supplied with the cage and replace them with natural perches made from non-toxic fruit tree branches. The lories will enjoy chewing these to pieces and the variation in width along the perch length provides good exercise for the birds' feet. Of course, the perches must continually be replaced as the bark is stripped and in order that they do not become too soiled.

Being active birds, and having a liquid diet, lories tend to squirt their feces out of the cage. An easy to wipe clean surface is recommended for these birds.

A wire bottom in your lory's cage will keep the feces directly away from your pet. A pull-out tray beneath this will facilitate removing the droppings that fall through.

The cage door must be of a good size so that you can place your hand into the cage with ease. Some doors are of the drop-down type which provide a landing platform for the bird. At least two good-sized feeding dishes should be a feature of the cage: one for the nectar and one for the dry mix or for fruits. A third dish will contain water. This is essentially for bathing in and must be of good size, but the lory will also drink from it. As with all food and water containers, they must be cleaned at least once every day. The base of the cage can contain peat, pet litter, or be lined with paper in order to soak up the feces.

Check out the door catch very carefully, for most parrots are adept at undoing these. It needs to be "parrot proof," and the best types are usually those which screw on. Do not be tempted to waste money purchasing any ornate type of cage. The best unit will be a simple box that is rectangular in shape and free of fancy bits that cost money and serve no purpose. Round cages are not desirable for birds though you will see plenty of them on the market.

A much better proposition where lory cages are concerned, is that you make, or have made, a unit which is enclosed on three sides and the top, leaving the

During warm weather it is safe to take your birds outdoors so they can enjoy sunshine and fresh air. Be sure to provide shade for the birds to retreat from the heat of the day.

front and the base in metal. Your pet shop will stock various sizes in parrot cage fronts. The appropriate size should be purchased in at least 19 gauge thickness and with 2.5cm holes. Below the weld- wire floor a pull-out tray containing the paper or pet litter should be placed. The weld-wire floor should also be on a pull-out frame so that it can be cleaned daily. The side walls and roof should be made using one of the coated woods which can thus be wiped clean with ease. Such a cage will dramatically reduce the amount of feces that are extruded out of the cage onto the surrounding floor area.

Many lory keepers have had success in breeding these birds in aviaries. This is a Blue-crowned Lory, *Vini australis*.

The bar spacing for lories should not be too far apart. They must be able to clamber about easily and should not be able to stick their head through.

STOCK SELECTION

The best advice one can give to a potential lory owner is to never to rush into buying this type of bird. It is best to shop around and see as many examples as possible. In this way both good and bad birds can be seen and you will be in a better position to judge the eventual stock acquired.

When you visit a bird farm, pet store, or breeder, the very first thing to do is to look at the conditions under which the birds are kept. If the cages are clearly too small or are in a dirty state, (making due allowance for the liquid nature of the feces of lories) make a quick exit. If a seller cannot maintain his/her own stock in first class conditions then they are unfit to provide you with any sort of advice or service. It happens that people often support such outlets simply because lories are not the most common birds so when one is on sale it tends to be purchased purely on the grounds of buyer convenience—a very poor criterion that only encourages the seller to try and buy more stock.

The Red Lory, *Eos bornea*, is very well established in aviculture. The needs of this species are simple; a basic diet of nectar and fruit will keep it happy and in good health.

SOURCES OF SUPPLY

To the average person the most obvious place to purchase a lory is from the local pet store. In the advertising sections of avicultural magazines you will find many breeders and pet stores listing the stocks they have available. With no national paper devoted to aviculture in Australia, one should make contact with the various bird societies, many of whom carry advertisements in their newsletters. Those living outside of Australia will find that they have a wider choice of species to pick from; those in Australia will find it virtually impossible to obtain "foreign" lories, which is to say species not indigenous to that continent.

If you have never owned birds before, then it is clearly beneficial for you to have an experienced bird keeper with you when you select stock. Even if he/she has not owned lories before, they may well have kept other parrot species and will be

Although some lories may be able to cohabitate, most cannot and should be housed separately.

aware what a healthy bird should look like and may know which are the best dealers to purchase birds from.

PRICES AND AVAILABILITY

Lories are not inexpensive birds so one must be prepared to pay out quite a lot of cash for even the so-called popular species. Of the 55 species only about 15 will be available and only half this number will be seen on a regular basis in dealer ads. These are not birds that you can just purchase whenever you like, and the amount of time spent searching for the right species and for breeding birds is to be regarded as the normal situation.

SEXING

Obviously, in any species that is costly it is very important to know the sex of the bird(s) one is purchasing, and birds of known sex will generally cost more than those of unknown sex. Likewise, the status of a pair of lories will be reflected by the price, so that a proven breeding pair will likely be the most expensive pair to acquire—and probably the most difficult to find because those with breeding pairs will tend to want to keep them.

The following abbreviations will often be seen in advertisements and so are explained.

Pr—A pair. No sex is implied but simply that the price is for two birds.

SP—A sexed pair. The birds are of known sexes but this does not imply they are a proven breeding pair or that they are even compatible.

Com—Compatible. A pair of birds which are known to get along with each other without fighting (all birds squabble but this is not fighting).

MP—Mature pair. Two birds that have reached breeding age. Such birds will have value to a breeder but will be of far less value to a pet owner who should seek young birds.

HR—Handreared. These are the best buy for pet owners but such rearing is a time consuming business, so expect to pay more for these birds. They will have no fear of humans and quickly adapt to the home environment.

Methods of sexing birds involve fecal hormone analysis in which microscopic examination can determine the ratio of sex steroids. The advantage of this method is that the bird is not subjected to stress and need not be taken from its home. It is also possible to determine the sex of a bird by studying its chromosomes. The sex chromosomes of a hen differ from those of a cock and by studying feather cells or other tissues, one can thus establish sex. The method is more popular in the USA than elsewhere but may well become the prime method worldwide in due course when its

All lories are gregarious creatures. They are commonly seen in groups of twenty or more in the tops of flowering trees. During feeding times, even larger flocks congregate.

Stella's Lorikeet, *Charmosyna papou goliathina*, the melanistic color phase. It appears that the normal color genes of this species are dominant, as red parents will always produce red youngsters, while black, melanistic parents may produce either color type.

cost is lower. In former times breeders used other methods to determine sex and these were based on anatomical observations, such as head size, pelvic size and so on, or were based on behavioral traits such as feather displays, mutual preening and nest building. None of these are reliable guides however because in a compatible pair situation, when both birds are of the same sex, it often happens that one will take on the role of the opposite sex. In the case of hens, it may well go as far as egg laying, but of course the eggs will not be fertile. Head size and similar observations are equally unreliable, though by considering a number of factors together, the experienced breeder will have a

Dusky Lory, *Pseudeos fuscata*. Most lories that live in aviaries can withstand temperate winters if they are properly acclimated.

better than 50/50 chance of determining sex.

HEALTH

It is not difficult to spot an unhealthy lory, or any bird for that matter. The first-time buyer with no experience at all need not worry about being sold a sickly bird, provided some common sense rules and observations are practiced. Even if the birds on display look fit enough, it may be that they are fresh arrivals and they will soon pick up any germs already in the establishment, or may already be incubating an illness.

A fit bird will have clear sparkling eyes; any which have sunken, are dull, or are weeping already have a problem. The nostrils, situated just above the upper mandible, should be the same size and show no signs of being swollen or congested with matter which could indicate a recent or current illness. The mandibles (bill or beak) should be correctly formed with the upper curving neatly over the lower and showing no signs of damage. Very thin birds should be avoided, especially those in which the breastbone appears prominent. This condition is called "going light" and can be very difficult, sometimes impossible, to cure; it indicates a dietary deficiency at some point in the bird's growth.

The feet should be in a good state with all four toes present.

A lory that is in good health will have clear eyes, good weight on its body, and tight feathers. This is a healthy Black Winged Lory, *Eos Cyanogenia*.

Although the keeping of lory species, such as this Rainbow Lory, is somewhat more complicated than other parrot-like birds, most hobbyists find that their beautiful plumage colors and their endearing personalities make them worth the trouble.

The anal region should not be caked with hard feces or badly stained, both of which indicate a problem. A fit lory will perch on one leg when sleeping or resting; it will place its head through 90 degrees and rest it between its shoulders, whereas a sickly bird will perch on both feet with its feathers fluffed out and may simply let its head sink into its neck; it may not even have the strength to remain on its perch and might be seen crouched on the floor in a corner. However, very nervous birds also tend to seek refuge in a corner, especially those that may have been recently imported.

Feather condition can be the most difficult aspect for the novice to judge. Sometimes an otherwise very fit bird can look in a pretty bad state simply because it has been subjected to feather clipping and may have been kept or transported in limited or overcrowded conditions. Its nectar food and liquid feces get all matted up on the plumage and it can appear in bad shape. A good bath will usually change the appearance dramatically and clipped feathers will be replaced at the next molt. Sometimes feathers will be missing, maybe on the head or on the chest. This can either be a self inflicted problem or other birds may be picking at it. Given this fact then, if a bird displays a large area of missing feathers to the chest (or any other region on the body) that bird should be overlooked.

When approached, a fit bird will be suspicious and move away from you, but a sick bird may be too ill to care. By considering a number of aspects one can easily avoid purchasing an unhealthy bird. Always try to collect any birds purchased, unless you really are sure of the reputation of dealers selling birds via mail-order, or breeders doing likewise. Most will guarantee live delivery but much after that you are on your own. If the bird arrives looking in bad shape, report this immediately to the seller and have a veterinarian check over the bird for you. Do not wait a day or two to see how things develop for in that time the bird could die and you would have little recourse against the seller if the condition was not reported on receipt.

TRANSPORTATION

When bringing a lory home, do so as early in the day as possible so it has time to settle in its accommodation after the journey. Transport it in a strong cardboard box which contains ample air holes. It will be less frightened if it is in a darkened situation so, if a cage is used, cover this with cloth and remove perches or place them very close to the floor. Remove feeder containers but of course have food available in the event the journey takes many hours.

Once home, place the bird in its temporary accommodation, feed it, and leave it alone until the next day so it can settle down without interference—especially from children where pets are concerned. Maintain the seller's feeding regimen for at least a week or so until the bird is familiar with you, thus content; dietary changes can be introduced gradually.

The postures of these Yellow-and-green Lorikeets, *Trichoglossus flavovirdis meyeri*, suggest that they may be pair-bonding.

QUARANTINE

Before placing any newly acquired lory in an aviary, the bird should undergo a period of

It is always a good idea to house new stock away from your existing stock for a few weeks to ensure that no illness exists. This is Meyer's Lorikeet, *Trichoglossus flavoviridis.*

The nominate species of the Papuan Lorikeet, C*harmosyna papou***.**

quarantine of about 21 days. During this period, any incubating illness should show itself. This is sound husbandry procedure which is neglected by many bird keepers who should know better. While in quarantine you have a better opportunity to study the bird at close quarters and can be sure it has settled down and changed over to your diet if a change is to be made.

Ideally, quarantine quarters should be spacious and well away from the aviaries, and they should be gently heated if the purchase has been made in the colder months. Lories are hardy birds but freshly imported stock must be acclimatized very carefully before it is released into an aviary.

An adult Violet-naped Lory, *Eos squamata*, with its two recently fledged youngsters.

Twenty subspecies of the Rainbow Lorikeet, *Trichoglossus haematodus*, are recognized. Many common names are used for different races. These include Green-naped, Mitchell's, Forsten's, Edward's, Wetar, Rosenberg's, Coconut, Red-collared, and Swainson's.

The temperature should be reduced to match that of the aviaries over a minimum period of 21 days (longer is far better) and only if the bird appears well and is feeding well should it be released into outdoor accommodation.

LONGEVITY

It is very difficult to say how long a lory will live because the lack of care or a proper diet seems to be the major cause of death rather than old age. A bird kept under ideal conditions will not necessarily outlive one kept under less than ideal conditions, though generally it should. Within imported captive stock, one cannot be sure just how old the bird was at the time of capture and birds react very individually to captivity. However, taking all these variables into consideration, a young lory given proper care and attention should live well into its teens and the larger species should exceed 20 or more years of age. With a greater understanding of the needs of these birds, it is most probable that the average life expectancy under captive conditions will steadily rise, though it is unlikely they will ever rival the known ages of the larger basically seed eating species such as macaws, cockatoos, or even Amazons and African Greys.

Little Lorikeets, *Glossopsitta pusilla*. Of the three species in this genus, this native of Australia is the least well-established in captivity.

FEEDING

Potential lory owners should visit as many other birdkeepers as possible. During such visits they should carefully make notes on the diets that are used to feed softbilled birds, especially lories. Likewise, a visit to the nearest zoological gardens that maintain lory collections will be well-rewarded, not only in seeing numerous species, but also in advice that the keepers will provide in respect to diets. The outcome of such discussions will be that no two owners feed quite the same diets to their lories. Two other aspects that become very clear are that nectar feeds must be prepared daily, and that cleanliness is doubly important with any bird species that requires a soft or liquid diet.

Lories are by no means difficult birds to cater to but they do require somewhat more attention than seed-eating parrots. Unless one is prepared to devote extra time to them, another species of birds should be acquired. However, given this little extra effort, the owner will be rewarded by the antics and color of these parrots in a way that few other species can offer.

Although the diet of lories and lorikeets is primarily of nectar and pollen, or imitations of these, it does not mean that they will not take other foods. This Yellow-and-green Lorikeet is enjoying what its owner has to offer.

ROLE OF FOOD

Food is used in many ways in the body, including building tissue, providing energy, insulating the bird from the cold, and protecting it from illness. The vast majority of parrots basically use a hard fuel, in the form of seeds, to provide their needs, but lories use liquid fuel. You wouldn't think of putting coal in your automobile, and in the same way one should never think of feeding lories hard food as their basic diet. The digestive system of seed eating parrots is so designed as to enable these birds to grind hard seed into pulp; they have very strong muscles in their gizzards. Lories do not possess such strong muscle and so they simply cannot cope well with seeds. It is true that they can digest seed if no other food is available but this results in very poor performance. Birds fed in this manner will never achieve optimal health nor are they likely to raise strong chicks—assuming they attempt to breed in the first place. It is important that this aspect of lories be fully understood.

TYPES OF FOOD

Food may be divided into three broad groups and are as follows:

Proteins—These are used to build tissue and muscle. They are vital to young birds. Rich sources of protein are meats, cheeses, milk, meat extracts, fish, certain seeds, and pollen. It is the pollen which lories are "designed" to harvest and absorb, as indicated by their brush-tongues which can reach into flowers to extract it.

Carbohydrates—These are used as an energy fuel needed in muscular action. They consist of sugars, which are more easily broken down to release energy than proteins. They are also much more plentiful in the world than proteins, and rich sources are seeds, plants, cereal crops, and fruits. A further source is nectar found in the flowering plants and it is this source that lories utilize.

Fatty Acids—These are converted into insulation material and are needed by the body in many other ways too. They transport materials via the blood stream and are essential to

A Blue-streaked Lory, *Eos reticulata*, sampling a nectar mix containing fruit.

For these Red Lories, *Eos bornea*, apple and orange have been impaled on the perches.

normal body cell metabolism. Rich sources are meats, butter, lard, cheeses, seeds, and milk. Fats, it will be noted, are often found in association with proteins.

Beyond these three major groups of food, vitamins and minerals are also needed by the body in very small amounts. They are especially found in fruits and vegetables, but all foods contain them in differing quantities. As long as a bird is given a well-balanced diet, it will receive its needed quota of vitamins and minerals.

The final food requirement of all living organisms is water. This may be provided in its obvious form—from the tap, or from streams, rivers and so on—or it may be extracted from other foods, such as fruits and vegetables, which themselves are made up essentially of water. Animals which consume foods containing high percentages of water tend to drink little. Having a basically liquid diet, lories are not big water drinkers when compared to other parrots who live on basically dry food diets.

DIET CONSIDERATIONS

Because captive birds do not expend as much energy as birds in the wild, the carbohydrate content of the diet—nectar—need not be so concentrated that the bird is receiving more than it needs. If it is, then the excess will convert to fat. Excess fat will slow down correct body metabolism

A group of *Eos* and *Trichoglossus* lories gather on the feeding station, which contains a fruit mixture.

Lory food must be changed several times a day. Only put out enough for your bird for one feeding at a time, or remove it after the bird has fed. Due to its contents, it will quickly spoil if it is left out for too long of a time.

resulting in disorders, so that the bird will become ill and may even die.

There is no fixed amount or specific considerations of nectar that can be quoted that will suit any lory due to the fact that no two birds are alike or live in the same conditions. Each bird is an individual and its diet must reflect the conditions it lives under and its own level of activity. The rule of thumb is that nectar is always better given more diluted than over-concentrated. The more diluted will not harm the bird but over-concentrated may.

In the wild, a lory gains its proteins (pollen) and carbohydrates (nectar) from the many flower species it feeds on. Nectar diets represent the best substitutes for flowers we can provide and should contain the needed food types. In the wild, the species also eat a certain amount of over- and under-ripe fruits, as well as a quantity of insects. We cannot provide the exact species of fruits and insects (even if we knew them all for sure, which presently we do not) and so we must experiment and draw on the findings of others. The pollen requirements of birds will reflect, as with nectar, the various conditions discussed, as well as take into account the size of the lory.

Few wild birds consume exactly the same foods year round because, as the seasons come and go, the flower and insect species vary. Foods eagerly sought, such as insects, during the breeding season may be totally ignored during other times of the year. This changing pattern will be seen in captive stocks and it is important that we appreciate it. If we do not, we may find the diet lacking when the birds are ready to breed, or being wasted if the breeding diet is continued into the non-breeding period.

While we understand that a substitute food item is valuable to our birds, the birds themselves may not appreciate this fact, and may refuse to accept it. It is important therefore that every attempt is made to provide a range of foods in order to find one our particular birds find enjoyable. This may also mean a high degree of waste in the early days, but it is essential to continue offering a given item even if it is refused for quite some time; exactly when to withdraw it is anyone's guess. Once withdrawn, food items should be tried again at a later date when weather conditions may have changed.

Various diet suggestions are given in this chapter but an owner should never be afraid to experiment with different foods, providing of course there is

reason to believe the foods contain a needed ingredient and are not potentially harmful. Do not withhold an item because someone else tells you their birds have never been prepared to accept it. Every lory is an individual and some will enjoy foods many other lories would never eat.

Because lories are very social birds, their diet is greatly influenced by what they see others eating. A bird that is very choosy, due to its former Spartan diet, may change once it is in a collection that receives a wide ranging selection of foods. It need not be in the same aviary because it is enough that it sees adjoining birds eating a given item.

FEEDING TIMES

There are two important points to make in relation to feeding schedules: they must be regular— given at the same time(s) each day—and they must, especially with lories, take the prevailing weather conditions into consideration. The author happens to live in a very warm part of the world which means that nectar and milk quickly go sour so it must be protected from the year 'round sunshine and not left for the birds for too long. In colder climates, this problem will not be as bad and foods may be left throughout the day.

Lories are active for a good part of the day, but they peak in the early hours and late afternoon. These are good times to feed them. If this is not possible, then whatever time is chosen should be continued with and the birds will become accustomed to the schedule.

FEEDER POTS

The type of feeder dishes one uses will reflect the species. Large lories need strong containers such as crock pots or similar containers that they will not treat as toys. Small species can be given plastic or aluminum dishes that are hung from the aviary wire or fixed in the shelter. Nectar can be supplied in open dishes or, for small species, in glass or plastic automatic dispensers. All of these are available from your pet store which will have many designs and sizes to choose from. All feeder containers must be cleaned daily. Never just top up dishes and never leave nectar or softfood

mixes in dispensers for more than 24 hours as this greatly increases the risk of ill health through food contamination. Remember, lories feed on fresh food in the wild and will only take less than such food if they are forced to.

OBSERVE YOUR BIRDS

One should always be prepared to stay near the birds when they are feeding so one can see what quantities of food each bird normally eats. If, subsequently, an individual is seen to be eating less than its normal rations, this may be the first indication of an impending illness, and so the bird can be isolated for closer observation and individual attention. However, birds (like people), do have their "off" days and only

Pictured here are several lories feeding from a metal tray on the floor of an aviary.

experience can tell you when it seems appropriate to isolate stock.

NECTAR MIXTURES

Over the years the basic ingredients of nectar-pollen substitute mixtures have varied considerably. The general trend has been towards increasing the number of ingredients so that today a wide range of foodstuffs are featured in many lory menus. There has also been some shift of opinion in very recent years towards increasing the dry mix content of diets, as opposed to the long-held belief that the nectar should be predominantly liquid. Here we can look at a few mixtures used by leading breeders of lories, but first we can look at the many potential items that one can obtain for the mixtures. Often these will be found in most home kitchens.

Baby cereal foods of all types have long been a basic ingredient as has baby milk powder, evaporated, and condensed milk. Care must always be exercised in the addition of milks to mixtures in countries having year 'round high temperatures because the milk quickly sours. Porridge oats and similar soft flake cereals together with comparable body building health foods are further products that will make a useful base to a mixture. Beef extracts, high protein supplements (available from pet stores and druggists) and any of the meat-flavored baby foods will all provide the required protein content of the nectar.

The carbohydrate content can be supplied by using honey, powdered glucose, sugar, golden syrup, and of course any of the branded nectars available from pet stores. The cereal content will also feature a high carbohydrate rate, as will bread (wholemeal is best), cakes, cookies and the likes of these. If a given lory shows no particular interest in eating fresh fruits, these can be liquified and added to the nectar mixture, thus ensuring an adequate supply of vitamins. Alternatively, vitamins can be added in powder form; they are produced by many companies and sold in pet stores. A word of caution should be added in respect to vitamins: *If your birds already accept a varied diet mixture, which includes fruits and vegetables as well as wild plants (either in their natural state or liquefied), there should be no need to add vitamin supplements. To do so could create health problems because an excess of certain of these will upset normal bodily metabolism.* It is presently very fashionable to use such supplements, but they should be used only if you have good reason to believe your bird's diet may be lacking in them—in which case your birds will reflect this in some way. If so, discuss the matter first with your veterinarian who will no doubt be able to cite the exact vitamin, or group of these, which need to be added to the diet.

An alternative to the liquid mixes is a much drier mix which can include finely chopped fruits, plants, biscuits, vegetables, cereals, lard, and honey (the last

Goldie's Lorikeet, *Trichoglossus goldiei*. There are many commercial diets available from your local pet store that will meet all the nutritional requirements for lories.

two items being dissolved in a small amount of warm water and added to the dry mix). This mix will keep for a few days in a suitable plastic container in a refrigerator but be sure it is well thawed out before feeding it to the birds. A separate liquid nectar can be supplied. Of course, any of the branded soft foods produced for softbilled birds can also be moistened to make a thick soup recipe, to which honey or sweetened milk can be added. The main thing is to establish which foods your birds like and then add or subtract from the menu periodically in order to supply them with a change which they will often appreciate.

Some lories will take few fresh fruits while others relish them. On the whole, lories (indeed most parrots) are rather wasteful when eating fruits for they will take a few bites and then drop the item before picking up the next one. You may prepare a mixed fruit and vegetable salad, chopped into cubes, and this may prove less wasteful. Wild plants and flowers can be supplied as available and many will be relished. Wash all plants gathered from the countryside, and those which are homegrown but which may have been subjected to pesticides (you may not use such sprays but your neighbor might, and this can be blown onto your garden).

Seeds form only a very small part of the lories' diet so never attempt to make them "seed eaters." However, a variety can be offered and these include most of those normally available from your pet store. Generally, if the seeds are soaked in hot water for about an hour, this will soften them and make them easier to digest. The large lories will probably ignore very small seeds, but try them first because such seeds provide excellent occupational therapy to those birds which will eat them. Many much larger parrot species are very adept at coping with extremely small seeds.

Live foods, such as mealworms, can be offered to breeding birds. They will be much appreciated as they provide high protein to the chicks; at other times of the year such foods will likely be ignored. Dried insect mixes can be purchased and sprinkled into the dry lory mix. Although lories clearly enjoy sweet-based foods, they should not be given sticky toffee or other candies which are invariably full of artificial ingredients and with which the lory will have difficulty coping.

Lories enjoy their food so they always look forward to seeing if any extra tidbits are offered that day. They will readily approach their owners and may start to eat the food before one hardly has a chance to place it into position; for this reason they will quickly become tame—a characteristic common to many birds who have a softfood diet.

Giving a lory a nutritious treat is a wonderful way to supplement the bird's regular diet.

PET LORIES

Few birds make such endearing pets as lories. They are natural clowns and are extremely affectionate to their owners. Many would-be owners tend to steer clear from these birds due to the nature of their diet and their harsh calls which they are likely to voice periodically. Adding the potential damage a large lory can do to furniture, it can be seen that they are far from being suited to all house-holds. They are, in fact, suited only to those who are prepared to live with these potential problems. Indeed, most large parrots have similar drawbacks, and if other factors are also considered, such as the time demands a parrot puts on its owner, then it becomes clear that well over half of all parrots sold as pets will end up in unsatisfactory homes. Would-be pet owners should understand that lories are not ornaments or "light switch pets" that can be turned on or off simply when the owner wishes; they are a commitment in just the same way as is a child.

Lories are amusing birds that will thrill you with their antics.

Lories are very intelligent birds that need to be kept occupied for many hours at a time. They are very social birds. They need company either of their own kind or that of their owner. Left to their own devices, they will become bored and are then far more likely to inflict damage to property when let out of their cages. They may also start to pluck out their own feathers. Such habits can be difficult, if not impossible, to correct.

PURCHASING A PET

It is very important that any bird purchased as a pet be young. An adult bird will never be totally capable of making the transition to a pet. A hand-reared baby lory is by far the best option as a pet, but of course will cost more than an adult bird. The difference is certainly worth it and will be repaid time and time again.

One might see an adult pet bird advertised for sale. This may be a good buy, but is probably also equipped with potential problems.

This Black-capped Lory, *Lorius lory*, cannot go far away from its owner because it has a leg chain attached to it. Never leave your pet unattended while it is wearing a leg chain because it could easily hurt itself if it tries to jump off.

The bird may be very noisy, have a tendency to bite more than the average, or may be especially destructive to furniture. These are matters not apparent at the point of purchase, and such a bird is best acquired only if the seller is prepared to give a guarantee that he will take the bird back in the event it displays habits not pointed out when it was purchased. The time limit on such an arrangement should be restricted. If the bird is known to you, of course you will already know its virtues and faults.

WING CLIPPING

Wing Clipping is very helpful in taming any parrot-like bird. The feathers will grow back normal once the bird molts. Molting occurs every year, usually in the late summer. There are several advantages to wing clipping. It makes the initial taming easier because the owner spends more time actually handling the bird, and it restricts the bird's ability to fly so it is less likely to get far should it escape from your home. The disadvantage, however, is that should it get loose and be unable to gain flight, it could quickly be attacked by a dog or a cat. This situation could be avoided by practicing caution and supervision when the lory is out of its cage. An unsupervised lory should never be left alone. No matter how tame the bird is it will get into mischief when no one is around.

If an owner wishes to have the wings clipped only for the initial period it should be performed by an expert. It can be done in such a way that one cannot see the cut feathers. One can also stipulate just how much flight the bird is to retain by cutting less feathers off. In this fashion, the bird will be able to get airborne but cannot gain too much height. Sometimes it is better to trim only one wing of the bird to unbalance it so that it cannot fly at all.

SECURITY

The average home holds many dangers for a pet lory so due consideration must be made. The following are typical examples:

1. An open fireplace is an escape route, and a danger to the bird if it is lit.

2. Ensure that all electric cables are neatly hidden from the bird. If not in use, unplug all appliances. Parrots are nibblers and might easily be electrocuted if they have access to wires. Remember that unconnected cables could also be chewed by a lory thus making the cable potentially dangerous the next time it is plugged in.

3. Aquariums without canopies are an obvious source of danger to a lory. One could easily drown should it by chance land on the water.

4. A kitchen is really full of dangers. Boiling pans, gas ranges, frying pans, electric appliances, and so on. It is best to avoid having your pet lory in the kitchen.

5. Until your pet is aware of where all windows and mirrors are in your house, they should be protected with curtains so that

It will take your pet lory awhile to adjust to your handling it. After it does, however, it will not allow you a moment alone for it will always want to be pet.

the bird does not dash itself into the glass during its time spent away from the cage.

Many parrots eventually become friends with other pets, such as dogs or cats. The main relationship between a lory and one of these pets will be purely one of mutual acceptance for each other, rather than friendship. Never leave a pet parrot in a room with a cat or dog if the bird is loose, even if they are compatible. It needs only one over-excited moment and the bird could be badly injured (the other pet may also get a nasty bite in the bargain!). Young children must be taught that lories can inflict bad wounds. A young child should never be left unsupervised with a bird not securely locked in its cage.

The lory cage itself should be positioned in a draft-free site that allows plenty of early morning sunshine into the cage. At no time should a bird be caged so that it cannot escape the direct rays of the sun; this could be very injurious to its health. Parrots are very inquistive birds and this factor will determine where to place the cage. Another important point to remember is that one should never place a cage where objects and people can tower above the bird. Birds find this very intimidating and it will greatly slow down their taming process. Ideally, the cage should be about eye level or just above it. Make sure that the parrot can climb to a point in the cage that is higher than you if it so desires. A bird feels safe in

this manner and believes to be on equal terms with you. Of course, a very tame lory will not be frightened if you approach it from a higher standpoint, but even then, it will want to rapidly climb onto your arm and then your shoulder so it can stay at an eye-to-eye position with you.

TRAINING

The most important virtues of any animal trainer are love and patience. With these, amazing results can be achieved. The fundamental requirement of training a parrot is to gain its confidence in you. This cannot be rushed. Just how soon a lory will tame will reflect the amount of time you spend with it.

When initially introduced to its new home, the bird should be left alone for the first day or two. This means that you should go about your normal business, and only attend to the needs of the pet itself. This is the familiarity period when the lory is carefully watching your every move to determine just how dangerous you are to it's well-being. Once your pet is satisfied you are not a threat to its life, then it will allow you to approach the cage without it clambering to the furthest point away from you. At this time you can sit near the cage and read a book or listen to the radio, and talk quietly to the lory as it eats its food. Tempt it with tid-bits through the bars and when it is happy to take these you can develop matters further.

Open the cage door and allow the lory to come out on its own.

Three subspecies of the Chattering Lory, *Lorius garrulus*, exist. The nominate race is not the most commonly available of the subspecies, but it is available from time to time and is easily distinguishable by the lack of yellow on the mantle. Pictured here is L.g. *flavopalliatus*.

It most likely will leave its cage and explore the room. If it is given plenty of time, it may return to the cage of its own choice. If not, approach it slowly and place a perch below its chest so that it can step up and you may slowly walk back to its cage to put it away. Usually when fresh food or some type of fruit that is very appealing to the bird is placed in the cage it will enter. Whenever possible, avoid manually taking hold of the bird because this will frighten it and set back your relationship, though sometimes this cannot be avoided.

If a lory must be picked up by hand, the best method is to dim the lights and, when it is on the floor, throw a towel over it. Be aware that the larger species can bite quite hard so lift the bird with care by placing your hand over its back and securing its neck gently, but firmly. Once the lory is really accustomed to having its daily freedom, it will always go back to its cage without problem.

Lories are very inquisitive parrots, so if you are sitting reading a book or doing some paperwork, curiosity will eventually compel the bird to approach you to see what is happening. It will nibble at the paper, the book, pencil or any other item around and all the while its relationship with you will grow. When it eventually steps onto your arm it will nibble. Do not pull away because it will not be an intentional bite (even though it might hurt a little), but an exploratory action to test this new material. Parrots use their beak as a third hand and may do no more than brace it on you while they step up.

Once finger tame, your relationship with your lory will advance at a very rapid rate and soon your pet will be clambering all over you. It will give you over-affectionate nips at times, but keep in mind that these are truly signs of affection. Most people stop at this level of friendship, some wish to continue the training process by teaching the lory tricks. Lories are very intelligent and quickly learn to do many things. This sort of training is not covered in the scope of this book.

If your pet starts to bite you too hard while it is sitting on your hand, hold on to the bird's feet and pull your hand down with the bird on it, and yell "No!" at the same time. The bird will not really know what happened, but if this sort of unpleasant action follows every bite it tries to give you, it will associate it with biting and will stop. A bodily smack is a definite no-no; it will merely frighten the bird and not teach it anything of value. Likewise, any discipline must be at the time of offense. It is quite wrong to shout at a lory that has, in your absence, chewed some cherished item. If it was that precious to you, it should not have been left where the bird could get at it or knock it over. Lories are like children, they can be very naughty at times. Neither lories nor any other pet are ever convenient. One must be prepared to put a lot into the relationship in order to obtain a lot out of it.

TOYS

There are countless toys produced for parrots to play with. Some toys are not very suitable because of the potential dangers they hold. Any toy that has sharp corners or protruding edges should not be offered to your bird. Wooden toys may be used providing the wood is soft enough

A small pile of fruit tree twigs will amuse any parrot. Lories usually delight in shredding and in doing so, gain some small nutritional benefit from the toy. Wooden hoops and suitable cylinders will likewise fascinate lories, as will anything suspended in the cage. Mirrors offer no benefits at all to any parrot species; indeed they can create psychological problems for the bird and should be avoided.

This is a Goldie's Lorikeet, *Trichoglossus goldiei*, at 34 days old. Occasionally, artificial incubation or rearing must take place instead of natural to ensure the survival of a chick.

for the lory to chew on. Other items such as bells or very colorful toys seem to catch these birds' attention and keep them occupied for hours. A good investment from your pet store would be one of the many feeding stations or playgrounds that are currently available. Such toys are both practical and entertaining.

GENERAL CARE

Lories enjoy bathing very much. An adequate sized bathing facility should be offered to the bird. If one is not available, the bird's feathers will become dry, the colors drab, and the molt may be prolonged considerably. Under the proper conditions a lory will enter a molt and complete it within 6-8 weeks. A constant temperature that is not too warm, a proper diet, and having the proper humidity level in the house all help to keep the bird in good, healthy-feather condition, and will bring about a proper molt. On warm days, a pet bird will appreciate having its cage placed outdoors during light showers. Watching the bird from a distance, one can see it extend its wings in all directions in order to gain full benefit from the occasion. It will then devote time to preening itself and the result will be an immaculate looking bird. By using one of the sprays available from your pet store, you can treat your lory to a weekly lukewarm water spray to help keep its plumage in top condition.

Sometimes the nails of a bird may grow too long. In such cases they should be either filed or trimmed. Be sure that too much of the nail is not cut off. Birds have a blood vessel that runs in every nail, if this is cut it will bleed. Nail clipping is easier to perform with two people. One person should secure the bird and someone else should trim the claws.

When cleaning out the bird cage, always be sure that all traces of disinfectants are rinsed away with scalding hot water.

It is certainly advantageous to have a small light on during the night so that the bird can see in case it becomes frightened. Should the bird become frightened in a situation where it cannot see, it can bang against the side of its cage and hurt itself badly.

Given due consideration for its needs, and the application of common sense to management, a lory can reward its owner with years of pleasure and affection.

Nearly seven weeks old, these Yellow-and-green Lorikeets, *Trichoglossus flavoviridis*, are fully feathered but paler versions of the adult birds. The best age to purchase a lory as a pet is when it has just been weaned.

HEALTH CARE

Given correct accommodation and care, the average lory should experience no particular problem in respect to its health. The pet bird, living a more isolated life in relation to other birds, is probably less likely to be ill than is the aviary bird simply because it is isolated from other birds. Thus it is less likely to contract an illness from any other parrots or wild birds. Its problems, should it have any, will arise through its confined home and illness induced by stress or boredom, or through the mismanagement of its needs by an inattentive owner.

Johnstone's Lorikeet, *Trichoglossus johnstoniae.* Lories will remain their healthiest on a nutritious diet and housed in a cage with plenty of space.

It must be stressed that the average bird keeper is totally ill-equipped to treat a sick bird. Those that profess to do so take a great risk in trying to treat any other than very simple problems. Should one or more of your birds become ill, do not delay in contacting your veterinarian. Do not attempt to treat the bird and do not listen to the advice—no matter how well intended—of other birdkeepers who claim great knowledge on aviary diseases. Even highly trained veterinarians do not know all the answers to the diseases of birds, but their considerable training and knowledge of treatments may help to diagnose diseases.

Aviculturists should therefore concentrate on matters of husbandry and other areas of interest in which they can accumulate knowledge; they should be more concerned with prevention rather than treatment.

DIAGNOSIS

One reason why a bird keeper cannot treat a bird, other than for superficial cuts and similar problems, is that it is important to correctly identify the cause of a disease before one can administer a remedy. Diagnosis presumes a very detailed understanding of anatomy, physiology, bacteriology, chemistry, and many other sciences, as well as on the likely effect of administering a drug. Also it is necessary to know what should be done if the treatment fails to alleviate the problem.

The clinical signs of an illness may apply to a great number of diseases. The bird is obviously limited in how it can display a problem. For example, it may sit fluffed up on its perch, its eyes may weep, its feces may become really liquid or foul smelling, and it may clearly have difficulty in breathing. Each of these symptoms may be caused by a multitude of internal problems. There may be a single causal factor, though this would be unusual, and the likelihood is that a number of things have gone wrong and are part of a chain reaction. Sometimes a vet can treat a sick bird for a number of factors at the same time, however it may be necessary (and more prudent) to treat for one factor at a time. All in all, it can be appreciated just how difficult diagnosis can be, and invariably microscopy is required to identify causal bacteria. In some instances, you can only really be positive of the cause of an illness after the bird has died. And as many bacteria quickly depart from a dead host, even post-mortems are only valid within given time spans, depending on the nature of the disease.

The bird keeper can be of considerable help to a vet in diagnosing an illness, because any illness must have been preceded by certain conditions that allowed the malady to gain impetus in the first place. The observant aviculturist will be continually aware of any subtle changes in his or her stock, and whether these changes may have coincided with other events. For example, problems may have arisen after the introduction of a recently acquired bird, or after changing the supplier of one or more food items. Maybe a rodent was seen in the aviary, or maybe a fellow bird keeper who may have had problems with his or her own stock visited your aviaries. Bacteria can gain entry into an aviary by many different ways. Once bacteria has gained entry to the accommodations of a bird it does not automatically follow that the bird will become ill. Again all this depends on the strength of the bacteria, because the birds will have a natural immunity to many disorders. However, if the bacterial invasion coincides with other negative happenings, then the invaders are able to overwhelm the bird's defenses and illness follows. The bird may have become chilled, or overheated, or its food may have gone sour, and each of these factors weakens the bird's immune system making it susceptible to illness. If the bird is unable to fight off the attack, its defenses start to collapse at an ever quicker pace—this is all-out war and your pet, like you, is conducting a running battle with alien bacteria throughout its life.

By the time you are aware of your pet's bacterial infection it sometimes is too late. The first you know of this battle is when your bird is clearly losing; it shows visible signs of this by its symptoms. At this stage the bacteria obviously has a major advantage, because it has had time to develop without you

Do not allow your pet lory to nibble on plants about the house as most are toxic and your bird could suffer extreme consequences.

knowing. The ultimate outcome, therefore, rests on just how fast the nature of the bacteria can be identified and counteracted with treatment. If a wrong treatment is given due to incorrect diagnosis, this may result in a double blow to the bird. On the one hand it fails to arrest the build-up of disease bacteria, while on the other hand it might actually damage the bird's defenses and thus speed up its demise.

OBSERVATION

It can be seen how important it is to continually study your birds. By doing so you will be aware of what is normal, thus equally aware of any small movements away from normalcy. Often, birds may be showing signs that things aren't as they should be, but the owner in all likelihood may fail to see the signals until it is too late (i.e. the bird drops dead or is very ill). Observation is not just a case of looking at the birds, it also includes studying their behavioral patterns for indications of stress or crowding. A bird being bullied by another will be prone to bouts of stress and may subsequently fall prey to an illness that might not affect other such birds in the immediate surroundings. You cannot be exact in determining how many birds can be accommodated in the same aviary (or even in the same block of aviaries), so only by experience and observation can you ascertain when overcrowding is taking place.

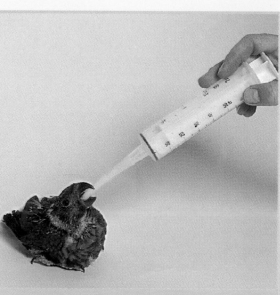

Hand-reared lories make wonderful pets. They know nothing except being cuddled and loved from practically right out of the egg.

REACTION TO ILLNESS

In spite of all precautions, a bird may still become ill due to unknown causes. If this occurs, a set procedure should be followed. First, the bird must be isolated from all other avians, and secondly, it must be given heat treatment but no form of medication. At this time, extra attention should be paid to the other birds, who even though may not appear ill, might be incubating the same problem. It does not follow that this is always the case but vigilance is the order of the day. Make as many notes as possible which will be of value to the vet:

What other birds are kept?

When was the last illness in the aviary?

Which were the latest additions to the stock?

What does the diet consist of?

When did one first notice the bird(s) was not well?

Have the symptoms changed and if so, at what rate of time is the illness progressing?

It may be helpful if you are able to gather sample feces from the bird and place these into a small plastic container so microscopy can be used quickly if needed.

Birds do not have sweat glands as we humans do so to relieve themselves of heat they will pant and hold out their wings.

If the bird has already been subjected to heat treatment, it would be unwise to then transport it to a vet's surgery, especially if this was any distance away. Pay the extra fees and have the vet make a house call—unless, of course, the nature of the illness requires very urgent attention and it is necessary to treat the bird in surgery.

HEAT TREATMENT

It is amazing just what effect heat can have on an ailing bird—

sometimes this in itself can bring about a complete recovery. Given this fact, every aviary owner should invest in basic heating equipment and an isolation cage. One can of course purchase one of many models of hospital cages, but these are not always without disadvantages unless one buys the really high priced units. The cost of equipment will be repaid if it saves a single bird. Therefore good husbandry necessitates that the correct facilities should be available well in advance— you should not wait until a bird is ill to get the necessary equipment.

CAGE

The isolation cage should be roomy enough for the lory to move about, but small enough to maintain a given band of temperatures. It is better to be constructed of a coated timber so that it can be thoroughly disinfected after each use. Perches should be placed low in the cage and food containers should be kept specifically for this cage and not shared with the aviary.

HEATING

The best way to heat the cage is with an infra-red lamp of the dull emitter type. These are preferable to heat lamps because they allow the light and heat intensities to be controlled as separate entities. You can purchase lamp stands which will enable you to position the infra-red unit to the desired distance from the cage. Also available are lamp clamps which can be fitted to the actual cage bars. It is certainly of benefit if there is a thermostatic control on the lamp so temperature can be regulated to required levels. As an extra safeguard , a separate thermometer can be placed in the cage, but protected from the lory's attentions. The heat lamp should be placed at one end of the cage thus allowing the bird to move away from the source if it feels uncomfortable. If it is unable to do this, it will certainly become more stressed at the very time you just don't need extra problems. Hospital cages with glass fronts do not provide this service.

This is a Dusky Lory, *Pseudeos fuscata*, at 37 days old. At this age lory chicks must be kept at a warm temperature or else they could quickly catch a chill.

LIGHTING

Much research has been done in recent years on the value of lighting as applied to animals. As far as birds are concerned, special lights are now available which can screen out harmful properties. It has been shown that light is important in helping to produce Vitamin D in birds' feathers. It has also been established that correct lighting will stimulate appetite, and this can be a vital factor in helping an ailing bird. Discuss the special fluorescent tubes now available with your pet store owner or with an aquatic supplier. However, before using very special lighting check with your vet about its suitability and be sure that the manufacturer's instructions are carefully followed. Remember also that all lights have a fall-off curve based on how many hours they have been used; in other words the fact that they appear to be working does not mean they are working to full specification and need to be replaced periodically. As with heat, it is beneficial if the light can be controlled, so a dimmer switch is a worthwhile extra.

FEEDING

Aviculturists vary in their attitude to feeding sick birds; some withdraw food altogether (other than liquid), while others merely withdraw certain items in the belief that these may be the items causing the problem. The author's view is simply to reduce the quantity of food given, not its variety content. A bird may quickly lose its appetite once it becomes ill, and withdrawing a given item may well be denying it the one item it either enjoyed or which is of greater benefit. If a lory stops eating

Clipping your lory's wings should be left to a professional handler or a veterinarian. It is important to know the proper way to hold the bird so that it does not bite you or become hurt.

altogether, this will certainly hasten the progression of its illness and one should do nothing that might encourage this situation. Of course, once the vet has examined the bird then his/her advice in respect of diet from that point on should be followed until the bird has fully recovered. Because the food will be situated in a higher than normal temperature it may be easily

spoiled, so the advice is to feed small amounts but on a more regular basis. Fortunately, where lories are concerned, many treatments can be given via the nectar food and so there is less risk that the bird does not ingest the required dosage than is the case with seed eating parrots where it must be given via the water—an unreliable method of treatment.

TEMPERATURE

The temperature range within the isolation cage is best at about 29-32°C (85-90°F). Once the bird is showing clear signs that it is recovering, the temperature can be reduced slowly over a number of days until it is back to that of the bird's usual accommodation. It must be stressed that quite often owners return birds to their aviaries prematurely, on the grounds that the bird has recuperated. The fact that the bird appears to be normal by no means ensures that its body is functioning normally, so treatments should be maintained as per veterinary instructions. It is far better to retain a bird in isolation for an extra day or two than to return it too early, when a relapse might occur.

TREATMENTS

Wherever possible, a veterinarian will supply antibiotics that can be taken orally via the nectar. Injections can be given and are certainly advantageous in many instances, but they are not without an element of risk when used on nervous aviary birds or recently imported stock. In such cases it is not uncommon for the birds to die from the combined shock of being caught up for examination and then injected. Treatment options should be discussed with the vet to decide on the best course of action. This again is further evidence of where steady home-bred birds can be superior to wild imports.

There is one course of preventive action that is justified with most parrots, especially where imported stock is concerned, and that is in regard to worms. Parrots tend to suffer from tapeworms so therefore it is worthwhile to de-worm fresh stock while it is undergoing its quarantine period. Likewise, there is advantage in repeating this procedure prior to the breeding season as it will greatly reduce the risk of worms being passed from the hen to the chicks.

EXTERNAL PARASITES AND WOUNDS

There are many forms of parasites that can host on a lory, but lice and mites are the most common. In both cases they are usually found on birds which live in unclean conditions, so obviously attention to hygiene should prevent the appearance of these unwanted guests. In the event they establish themselves, things will become apparent as the lories will be seen scratching themselves quite a bit. They will become restless and may not be able to sleep as they should and this may then induce further problems. In severe infestation cases, parasites will establish themselves in nest boxes and can prove so troublesome that hens have been known to abandon chicks; they cause anemia and the wounds made by the birds in trying to rid themselves of these parasites can result in secondary infection setting in. This might be worse than the original problem.

There are many products now available from veterinarians which will eradicate these pests. In some cases, treating one species of parasite will eradicate others as well. However, merely removing those on the bird is quite pointless because unless the parasites and unhatched eggs are killed at the source, they will obviously just reinfest the bird later. Perches should be destroyed and the entire cage or aviary of an infected bird carefully treated. Any crevices in wood are likely hiding places so it is important that all stock cages are treated, and nest boxes should be replaced periodically as a matter of routine.

Should a bird injure itself and start to bleed, carefully assess

This is a Scaly-breasted Lorikeet at one month of age. Baby lories grow very rapidly and in another four weeks this chick will almost be fully feathered and ready to leave the nest.

THE SPECIES

A species is a naturally occurring group of individuals that will freely interbreed in the wild state. They will produce offspring that resemble themselves. In many species, the members all look the same externally but in others they do not. The sexes may differ in appearance; when they are referred to as being sexually dimorphic, the species has two visual forms. While a species can readily be identified as such, it is possible to divide even this rank. Differences which are consistent enough to be perceived and warrant such division create a subspecies. A subspecies usually occurs where a natural barrier—such as a mountain range, a large stretch of water or an area of desert—prevents members of a former single population from breeding. Even within a subspecies one can see minor differences in appearance which can be regarded as geographic variations if they are consistent.

For all practical purposes, the average bird keeper will only be concerned with matters down to the rank of subspecies; indeed, in many instances they will be selecting and breeding birds only at species level. Because of this latter fact there has been a large degree of hybridization within aviculture. This may be acceptable at subspecific level, it has very little value at species

matters by inspection of the damaged area of the body. Small cuts will heal without problem so they need only to be cleaned and treated with a suitable antiseptic. If the wound is deep and bleeding rather badly, then wrap the bird in a towel so its movements are restricted, after which it should be transported to the vet for surgery as quickly as possible. Broken legs and wings can sometimes be reset so that the bird is no worse for the break; in other cases the break cannot be set into its original position so the bird will always show evidence of the accident. Apart from this, it will live quite happily and and will eventually adjust to compensate for the new position of the leg or wing.

rank because it merely creates problems down the line in trying to retain pure strains of a given species. Likewise, retention of a species is made difficult if a number of breeders hybridize stock simply because it is convenient to do so, because they are unable to obtain sexes of the same species. A basic understanding of taxonomy as applied to the lower ranks is thus beneficial in appreciating the need to keep species (or subspecies where possible) distinct.

NOMENCLATURE

Lories can be referred to by one of two types of name so each species will have one or more common names and a scientific name. The common name is the one coined within an area or given country, but the scientific name is applied on a worldwide basis. As an example, the Rainbow Lorikeet is also known as the Blue Mountain or Blue-bellied Lorikeet, depending where you live, but its scientific name of *Trichoglossus haematodus* is totally international. The scientific name is composed of two parts, the first indicating the genus while the second identifies the type of bird within that genus; together the two words identify the species. If there are one or more subspecies of a species this is indicated by adding a third word to the species name; the binomial name thus becomes a trinomial.

TREATMENT OF SPECIES

In the following text, the species will be given their usual common name and other names (synonyms) by which they are also known. The terms lory or lorikeet will also be used in this section. The comments given for the genera or species are necessarily of a basic nature and they will provide the platform onto which more detailed knowledge can be added through both practical experience and reference.

SPECIES REFERENCES

Experts may differ on the status they accord to given species of bird. One authority may regard a bird as a species whereas another may feel it is merely subspecific to an existing species. One person may assign a lory to a given genus but another person may not feel this is appropriate. This situation is possible, and quite in order, because such decisions depend upon the importance of features used in determining status. New information necessitates constant re-evaluation of previously held thoughts, so that taxonomy is never static but always subject to change, thus reflecting individual as well as collective ideas on the relationship of one species to another. In this work, the author has followed the listings given by Richard Howard and Alick Moore in *A Complete Checklist of the Birds of the World*, 1984 printing. Where applicable, additional common names have been added if they are in popular use from one country to another, and therefore likely to be found in advertisements.

The Black Lory, *Chalcopsitta atra*, exhibits an area of bare skin around the lower mandible; a characteristic common to all species of this genus.

GENUS *CHALCOPSITTA*

There are four members of this genus but none are popular or readily available in aviculture. Those which are offered for sale are very expensive. The Black Lory, *C. atra*, is an imposing bird of some 31cm (12 in). Best kept in aviaries where the sunlight will reflect purple or deep red from the apparently black plumage. Those who have kept the species all comment on its extremely affectionate nature once tame. However, it can also be a very noisy bird. It has been bred on numerous occasions but losses have been higher than is normal for lories as a whole.

Duyvenbod's lory, *C. duivenbodei*, is best seen in a large aviary. Like others in the genus, it can be noisy but makes

Duyvenbode's Lory, *Chalcopsitta duivenbodei*. This species is rarely seen in captivity. Recently there has been a greater number showing up in aviculture.

a most beautiful aviary bird for its colors are most attractive when it is in flight. Though known in aviculture since the early years of this century, it was not until the 1970s that breeding took place.

The Yellow-streaked Lory, *C. sintillata*, has followed a similar path as the others of the genus in that, after being imported many years ago, it vanished from the bird scene until the 1970s. At that time its price became very high but fell back dramatically before rising again. Today it commands its true worth.

The Cardinal Lory, *C. cardinalis*, is very rare in aviculture. All the birds of this genus are native to New Guinea and its offshore islands, and all exhibit a naked area of skin below the lower mandible. None are sexually dimorphic.

GENUS *EOS*

Six species are housed within this genus and size in the genus ranges from 23-31cm (9- 12 in) and the members are non-dimorphic. They have been very popular aviary subjects for many years. The various species are native to the islands of Indonesia and New Guinea.

Red Lory, *Eos bornea;* 25-31cm (10-12 in). Distribution: Ambon, Buru, Ceram, and other islands of the Moluccas that are found between Papua New Guinea and Indonesia. Comment: The Red Lory is easily the most popular member of the genus and was once possibly the most frequently

Blue-streaked Lories, *Eos reticulata*, 42 days old. Blue-streaked Lory chicks spend a fairly long time in the nest, up to 14 weeks! Hand rearing is often necessary because the parent birds become unreliable in the latter part of the rearing.

The Violet-necked Lory, *Eos squamata*, gets its name from the violet collar that extends around its neck.

Dusky Lory, *Pseudos fuscata;* 25cm (10 in). Distribution: Extensive throughout Papua New Guinea and neighboring islands. This species has features that would suggest it is a halfway stage between the lories of *Eos* and the lorikeets of the next genus to be discussed, which it somewhat resembles in looks. Rare until the 1970s, the dusky has proved a prolific breeder and is thus well established in aviculture, though it is not a species one will see too often in pet stores as it lacks the vivid colors that retailers prefer to keep in stock.

Red Lory, *Eos bornea.* Natural branches that are placed in your bird's cage should be free of all chemicals and sprays.

available lory. It is a good species for the beginner to start with, though its somewhat raucous voice might prove a problem to some owners. It remains one of the least expensive species of the family though in recent years it has increased in price.

Less readily available, though not actually rare, are the Blue-streaked lory, *E. reticulata* and the Violet-necked or Naped Lory, *E.squamata.* These species show more black and blue in their plumage and are slightly smaller than the Red Lory.

GENUS *PSEUDEOS*

This is a monotypic genus, meaning that it contains just one species.

The Dusky Lory, *Pseudeos fuscata*.

GENUS *TRICHOGLOSSUS*

Containing some 10 species, this is the second largest genus in the family Loriidae. One member, the Rainbow Lorikeet, is probably the most popular lorikeet in aviculture at this time, and with 20 subspecies has more forms than any other parrot. The birds of the genus range in size from 17-31cm (6-12 in) and all display the long tail feathers associated with lorikeets. None are sexually dimorphic. Certain members have proved extremely prolific breeders, so this is reflected in their prices. Others remain quite rare in captivity.

Ornate Lory, *Trichoglossus ornatus*. The beautiful coloration this species displays has made it enticing to hobbyists.

Ornate Lorikeet, *Trichoglossus ornatus;* 25cm (10 in). Distribution: Celebes and its offshore islands. This species is seen less frequently than in past years, though it is a reliable breeder which normally lays 2-3 eggs. A most attractive species, the Ornate Lorikeet is well recommended to those just starting with birds of this family.

Rainbow Lorikeet, *Trichoglossus haematodus;* 26-31cm (10-12 in). Synonyms: Blue Mountain Lory, Swainson's Lorikeet, Bluey, Blue-bellied Lorikeet. In order that the novice is not perplexed by the names applied to this species, it should be stated that while the term "Rainbow" has application to the numerous subspecies that, collectively, may be referred to as Rainbows. It is more customary within aviculture to apply specific common names to the various subspecies. The Rainbow Lorikeet is the subspecies *T. h. moluccanus* of Australia, while the nominate race, *T. h. haematodus*, is known as the Green-naped Lorikeet. Potential owners, seeing birds advertised as Rainbows, are advised to check further with the dealer selling the birds as to which subspecies is actually being offered for sale, if this is of importance to the buyer.

Distribution: East, from Bali in the Lesser Sunda islands to the Pacific islands of Vanuatu (formerly New Hebrides) and New Caledonia. North and eastern Australia and south to Tasmania. Not only is this species quite spectacular to look at, but it is also one of the most delightful of pets when tamed. Add to this its excellent breeding record and surely one has what must be one of the most desirable of all parrots. Because it is well established in captivity, it has the further benefit of being modestly priced—a true avian jewel, well recommended to first time lory owners. The differences between the numerous subspecies range from slight to very marked, and availability of the various subspecies is equally variable.

Scaly-breasted Lorikeet, *Trichoglossus chlorolepidotus;* 24cm (9 in). Synonyms: Gold and Green Lorikeet, Greenie. Distribution: NE Australia. Comment: Mutant color forms have appeared and the species has hybridized with other members of the genus.

Goldie's Lorikeet, *Trichoglossus goldiei;* 19cm (7 in). Distribution: Central Papua New Guinea. This pleasant looking bird is attractive without being in any way an eye-catcher. Comment: Goldie's Lorikeet was virtually unknown to aviculture prior to the late 1970s but since then has become so well-established that it is now the most frequently bred lorikeet. Goldie's is not like other members of this genus for it does not have the playful nature of the species so far discussed. Further, it does not so readily roost in its nest box. It is presently the least expensive lorikeet species, and given its hardiness and prolific breeding records is likely to remain so into the future. As

In its native New Guinea, Goldie's Lorikeet, *Trichoglossus goldiei*, is not a plentiful species.

The Scaly-breasted Lorikeet, *Trichoglossus chlorolepidotus*, has been rare in aviculture outside Australia, but within its own country its populations are secure and it has been widely kept and bred by bird keepers.

mutational forms start to appear, this species will most certainly gain even greater popularity. It is well recommended to those starting with this family of parrots. The diet comprises the usual nectar mixture but fruits and soaked seeds will also be taken.

Varied Lorikeet, *Trichoglossus versicolor.* **Members of this species frequent the tropical lowlands of northern Australia.**

Two related species that are not unlike the Goldie in size and color are the Varied Lorikeet, *T. versicolor,* and the Iris Lorikeet, *T. iris.* Neither of these delightful little lorikeets is readily available. Although the small lorikeets are hardy, one should not take this to mean they can endure very cold winters, at which time it is better to offer them indoor shelter if possible. It is worthy of note that Iris Lorikeets owned by the parrot authority Rosemary Low continued to produce fertile offspring when at least 13 years old—indicating that the small species, if well cared for, do enjoy very good longevity which could well pass the 20 year mark.

GENUS *LORIUS*

This genus contains eight species, all of which have short, rounded tail feathers. The beak is broad and less pointed than in other similar genus, but generally they have an appearance not unlike that of the *Eos* genus, the green of the wings being the obvious difference to this latter genus of lories. The major drawback of *Lorius* species likely to be available is their rather harsh voices. On the positive side, they make quite delightful pets if hand-reared or acquired at a young age, and may become quite passable talkers imitating various sounds, including the songs of other birds.

Black-capped Lory, *Lorius lory;* 31cm (12 in). Distribution: Papua New Guinea. One of the more popular and available members of the genus, this must, however, be viewed against a background in which none of the *Lorius* species can be considered common. There are some six subspecies which differ in detail placement of their colors. The species has proved to be a reliable breeder.

Less readily available, but equally desirable, is the Purple-capped Lory, *L. domicellus.* This is

The Black-capped Lory, *Lorius lory,* although very popular, has failed to become established in aviculture.

slightly smaller at 28cm (11 in). In color it has a more extensive area of red, there being no blue on the nape or the abdomen; blue is restricted to the thighs. The beak is more yellow than orange.

Chattering Lory, *Lorius garrulus*; 31cm (12 in). Distribution: Numerous small islands of the Moluccas, Indonesia. The Chattering Lory is a long-time favorite and probably the most readily available member of the genus. It is still only modestly priced when one compares its beauty with that of other, less colorful, parrot species which command considerably more money. Like most species of lories, the Chattering is not only a confiding pet but is also a really amusing bird that will adopt all

sorts of positions in order to look at things. This and related species are great lovers of bathing and should be supplied with a more substantial facility than just a pot dish. If this is done, then the bird will flap and play about in the water in a much more exuberant manner than one would normally associate with birds. The great benefit of this is that the bird's plumage really will remain in immaculate condition.

GENUS *PHIGYS*

This monotypic genus contains the species *Phigys solitarius*—the Collared, Solitary or Ruffed Lory. It is a small bird of some 20cm (7 in) which is native to the Fiji islands. It is an avicultural rarity so will be most unlikely to appear

The Chattering Lory, *Lorius garrulus,* is known for the strange gurgling sounds it makes while eating.

on any dealer listings. Only a handful of collectors have ever owned the species.

GENUS *VINI*

There are five species in this genus and all are quite exquisite avian gems. However, like the preceding species, aviculturists would indeed be lucky if they were ever to see living examples, let alone have the opportunity to own them. The value of these birds would be very substantial indeed, so to most of us they will only ever be beautiful pictures seen in books.

The Tahiti Blue Lory, *Vini peruviana*, is well known as one of the rarest and most beautiful of lories.

The Collared Lory, *Phigys solitarius*, is most often referred to as the Solitary or Ruffed Lory.

GENUS *GLOSSOPSITTA*

There are just three species within this genus and they are small birds with a length of 15-23cm (6-9 in). Native to Australia, they were exported in past years but, due to lack of knowledge of feeding techniques, were never established in aviculture. When the Australians placed export bans on their wildlife, this effectively terminated non-Australian-keeping of these birds. Even within Australia only one species, the Musk Lorikeet, *G. concinna*, could be regarded as plentiful in aviary collections.

The Blue-crowned Lory, *Vini australis*, is virtually unknown in aviculture.

GENUS *CHARMOSYNA*

With some 14 species and 13 subspecies, this is the largest genus in the family. However, none of the species are readily available, and are almost unknown to most aviculturists other than being featured in books or occasionally seen in zoological gardens. Most have been kept at one time or another but as they are native either to small islands or to dense forest regions, supplies were never plentiful. Export bans mean that it is unlikely that we shall see many ever again appearing on dealers' lists, or at least not until policies are worked out that might allow the export of restricted numbers for avicultural purposes. While a number of the species are

rather plain-looking birds in which green is the predominate color, others are quite beautiful, displaying red, green, blue, violet, black, and mixtures and shades of these. In size, the species range from small birds of 13cm (5 in) to elegant avians attaining up to 41cm (16 in). Two examples of the genus are cited here, one at each end of the size range, and which are still in collections.

Fairy Lorikeet, *Charmosyna pulchella;* 13cm (5 in). Distribution: Papua New Guinea. The subspecies *rothschildi* is the one usually seen in aviary collections. The species is sexually dimorphic and the hen has yellow patches on the sides of the rump, the latter being a dark blue in the

In the Red-flanked Lorikeet, *Charmosyna placentis*, sexual dimorphism is marked.

The Purple-crowned Lorikeet, *Glossopsitta porphyrocephala*. This highly attractive lorikeet is rarely available outside Australia, although it has been widely kept within its own country.

male. These are not birds that can be regarded as hardy in temperate climates and should be provided with heated quarters in all but the warm summer months. This is certainly not a species the novice should attempt to own, even if it were available, but is certainly the sort of lorikeet most would aspire to breed. A true gem, it has an affectionate nature, is gentle, is not noisy and is stunningly beautiful.

Papuan Lorikeet, *Charmosyna papou;* 41cm (16 in). Distribution: Papua New Guinea. This species is very interesting as it also exhibits a melanistic form which is a shiny black. The subspecies *C. p. stellae*, Stella's Lorikeet, is much the more widely kept and as in the previous species

discussed, dimorphism is seen, the female having yellow to the sides of the rump as well as to the lower back. Immatures can be sexed as they feather, for the males have red backs while that of the female is yellow. The black forms have red in the males and green in the females on their back areas.

GENUS *OREOPSITTACUS*

This monotypic genus contains the single *O. arfaki*, commonly known under the names of Whiskered, Arfack Alpine, or Blue-cheeked Alpine Lorikeet. It is native to Papua New Guinea

The Musk Lorikeet, *Glossopsitta concinna*, is named for the musky odor it exudes.

Papuan Lorikeets, *Charmosyna papou*, the red color phase.

where it inhabits altitudes of 8-12,000 feet. A small bird of 15cm (6 in), it is unknown to aviculture but has the unique distinction among all parrots of having 14 tail feathers; all others have but 12.

GENUS *NEOPSITTACUS*

This genus contains two species and both are extremely rare in aviculture. Native to Papua New Guinea, they live at mountain altitudes and appear to live on a diet which is mainly of seeds—most unusual for this family of parrots. In spite of the rarity of the species, it does not follow that examples will necessarily command vast sums.

The species just mentioned was *N. musschenbroeki*—Musschenbroek's Lorikeet. This species has a length of 23cm (9 in). The closely related Alpine or Emerald Lorikeet differs from the nominate race in having a greater area of red on the underbelly. The Emerald Lorikeet has a length of 18cm (7 in), so it is somewhat smaller.